Infant Massage
from Head to Toe
A Basic Guide to Infant Massage

Alicia Jackson
Certified Massage Therapist
Certified Infant Massage Instructor

Published by Bee Creative, Inc.
Oklahoma City, Oklahoma
Copyright © 2014 by Alicia Jackson

Distributed by Lightning Source, Inc.

For ordering information or special discounts for bulk purchases, please contact Lightning Source, Inc., at 1246 Heil Quaker Blvd, La Vergne, TN USA 37086 (615) 213-5815.

Publisher's Cataloging-In-Publication Data
(Prepared by The Donohue Group, Inc.)
Jackson, Alicia, author.
Infant massage from head to toe : a basic guide to infant massage /
by Alicia Jackson -- First edition.
pages : illustrations ; cm

ISBN: 978-0-615-94698-6

1. Massage for infants--Handbooks, manuals, etc.
2. Infants--Care. 3. Parent and child. I. Title.

RJ53.M35 J33 2014

615.8/22/0832

Cover, interior design, and composition by Christina Hicks
Edited by Callie B. Ferguson
Printed in the United States of America
13 14 15 16 10 9 8 7 6 5 4 3 2 1
First Edition

Dedication

This book is dedicated to my beautiful daughter, Emily Caroline Jackson.

Emily, you are the love of my life. You have grown into a very beautiful girl, and you inspire me every

day. I am truly blessed to have you as my daughter. You are a true gift from God. I love you!

To my parents, who have loved and supported me every day of my life.

Thank you for believing in me and having continued faith in me.

And last but not least, my Savior, Jesus Christ.

I give Him all the praise and glory!

Important Notice

This book is written by a Certified Massage Therapist and Certified Infant Massage Instructor. All advice and techniques demonstrated in this book are recommended by a certified professional.

The ideas, procedures, and suggestions contained in this booklet are not intended as a substitute for consulting with your physician. All matters regarding your child's health require medical supervision.

Always seek the advice of a trained health professional with any questions you may have regarding a medical condition and before beginning a massage. Proper medical attention should always be sought for specific ailments, as massage is intended to be supplemental, holistic treatment.

Introduction

I have always had a heart's desire to perform massage therapy, and I have been a certified massage therapist and certified infant massage instructor since 2007. I've also been a licensed esthetician (skin care specialist) since 2002. I first heard about infant massage while in massage therapy school; so I researched it, prayed about it, and God led me to practice it.

I've been working for a local women's hospital since 2008, which has been very rewarding because I get to help women feel better at both the prenatal and postnatal stages. I'm also constantly multitasking. I perform in-hospital as well as outpatient massage, and I teach parents infant massage and also offer skin care services. I meet and work with so many people, and hopefully my knowledge and practice of massage therapy helps them feel better. I have truly been blessed with my work.

I am also the proud mother of one beautiful daughter, Emily, and I often teach parents things I wish I knew when she was a newborn! If there's one thing I hope all parents take away from this book, it's the tummy massage. It usually takes the newborn tummy six to twelve weeks to figure out the flow of the colon, but by implementing tummy massage, you can hopefully lessen any digestive issues early on, making both you and your baby much happier!

I hope you find this book useful and informative, and don't forget that even though infant massage is recommended for babies from birth to twelve months, you can massage your baby for as long as he or she permits it and remains helpful! May you be blessed.

—Alicia Jackson
Certified Massage Therapist
Certified Infant Massage Instructor

Purpose

The purpose of infant massage is to promote healthy, loving touch. Since touch is one of the most developed senses at birth, your newborn baby's *lifeline* is touch. The more you offer healthy, loving touch the more your baby will thrive. Infant massage provides important tactile stimulation as well as relaxation and regulation of the respiratory, circulatory, and digestive systems. The soothing effects of infant massage help to ease a gassy tummy and can be very beneficial for your baby. A healthy, loving touch is good for everyone but especially for infants, who are new to the world and need reassurance from someone special.

Benefits

Benefits of infant massage for the infant include:

- Promotes a loving, secure, bonded relationship

- Is relaxing, calming, and soothing

- Helps regulate digestive system and may also reduce gas, colic, and constipation

- May increase weight gain

- Decreases stress hormones (cortisol)

The key to a happy baby is a happy tummy! When your baby has a happy tummy:

- Feeding times are more scheduled

- You'll both experience longer sleep patterns. If baby is sleeping longer, Mom and Dad are sleeping longer. Mom, if you're sleeping more, your hormones will come back sooner.

- It improves baby's immune system.

Benefits of massage for the massage giver include:

- A loving, secure, and bonded time with the infant.

- Improved parent-infant communication.

- Improved understanding of each other.

- Ability for parents to understand and respond to baby's nonverbal cues.

- Increased confidence and handling skills.

Massage therapy can trigger many physiological changes that help infants and children grow and develop. Another benefit of infant massage is learning to communicate together through:

- Eye contact

- Saying your baby's name

- Saying, "I love you."

- Singing to your baby

These four are strongly encouraged throughout the massage.

Who Needs to Know Infant Massage?

The practice of infant massage dates back to ancient times. It's a physical experience of quality time between the parents and the child as well as with any significant other in the baby's life. Obviously, mothers and fathers should know infant massage, but others can include grandparents, guardians, and caregivers.

Understanding Your Baby

Each baby has his or her own unique way of communicating, and you will find it easier to take care of your baby when you can understand what baby is trying to communicate to you in the various stages between sleep and activity. Understanding your baby's behavior will help you get to know your baby better and know the best time to feed your baby, play with him or her, and give a massage! Below are descriptions of the most common infant states and cues to help you learn to understand your baby.

Infant States

Knowing the subtle variations between asleep and awake in your baby is critical to determining the best times to give infant massage.

- Quiet Sleep: Baby will lie still, with no eye movements and smooth breathing patterns. He or she will be very hard to wake up.

- Active Sleep: Baby will experience some body and facial movements. The eyelids may flutter. This may be your baby's dream state.

- Drowsy: Baby's eyes may open and close. They are heavy lidded and glazed. This state occurs just before falling asleep.

- Quiet Alert: Baby is awake, alert, and may take a gazing or staring interest in things nearby, making cooing sounds. This is the best state to give infant massage; the key is to go slowly and allow your baby to relax.

- Active Alert: Baby makes more body movements, is sensitive to noise, and might be hungry. Ask yourself, *Is my baby hungry? Does he or she need a diaper change or a nap?* This is not a recommended time to begin infant massage.

- Crying: Baby will cry, grimace, and make a lot of body movement. Crying means your baby needs to be soothed with movements like rocking, swaying, or bouncing.

- Most commonly missed cue, especially in newborns: Hungry vs. gassy Always ask yourself, *When did baby feed last? Could he be hungry? Does she have a dirty diaper? Or is it just gas?*

Infant Cues and Behavior

Engagement and disengagement cues are your baby's way of communicating with you what he or she wants. Most of these cues are nonverbal in the early months of life, but knowing about these cues will make it much easier and more enjoyable to provide care for your baby, including giving a massage.

- Engagement means your baby wants to be held and will attract you. Baby will reach out to you, smiling, cooing, and making eye contact and giving you a winning smile. His or her excitement will be apparent with waving arms and legs.

- Disengagement means your baby wants to withdraw from being with you. Baby will turn his or her head away and might start crying. Fussiness or pulling away means your baby is overwhelmed and needs a break from interaction.

When Is a Good Time to Give Infant Massage?

To offer infant massage doesn't mean you have to give a full-body massage every time. You can choose to just do a quick tummy massage or soothe your baby with a short back rub. The choice is yours. The infant state of *quiet alert* is a good time to offer infant massage. Quiet alert is when your baby is awake but quiet and still, taking a gazing, staring interest in things nearby. Other times for infant massage are early in the morning, after bath time, or just before bedtime. You will learn when the best time should be by your baby's response.

Infant massage is unique to each parent, and it's important to follow your baby's likes and dislikes. Holding your baby and applying massage will create a sense of security and a loving bond, and you will learn over time what your baby prefers. Here are some basic guidelines to get you started:

1. *Do not* massage your baby immediately after feeding or when your baby is hungry. Wait thirty to forty-five minutes after feedings to perform a full-body massage.

2. *Do not* massage your baby if he or she has a fever.

3. *Do not* massage your baby if *you* are tired, stressed, rushed, or angry. This is not a good time because your baby will sense this from you, and the baby will become stressed.

Do You Need to Ask Permission?

Yes! It's just as if you are asking if your baby is hungry or wants to play. Parents need to ask permission for anything they do with their children, expecially massage. This gives your baby a chance to express his or her feelings and emotions. Prior to beginning the massage, ask your baby for permission to give him or her a massage. Here are some guidelines and tips:

- Make eye contact with him or her, and ask, "Do you want a massage?" or "Are you ready for a massage?"

- Having lotion or oil in the palm of your hands and rubbing them together in a circular motion is also a sign of massage.

- Watch your baby's body language to know whether he or she is engaging or disengaging. Example; watch for a smile on baby's face or crying.

Where Is a Safe Place to Offer Infant Massage?

Areas such as your bed or a changing table are not recommended for infant massage because the baby could roll and fall from a height. The safest place to offer full-body infant massage is the floor. Make a pallet with blankets and quilts, and provide two pillows: one for you to sit on and one to support your back.

Keeping your back straight, bend forward at your hips, stretching your legs out in front of you. With your legs apart, you can work with the baby between your legs. You may even choose to prop your baby on a pillow to have a more upright position. Or you can sit on your knees and work with the baby in front of you. If you choose to massage with your baby's diaper off, you'll need to place a thick towel under your baby.

What Should the Environment Be Like?

- Temperature: Make sure the room you are massaging in is warm. Babies are not good at regulating their body temperatures. Use a blanket to swaddle your infant if he or she gets cold.

- Light: It's best for the room not to be too bright. Use a lamp or nightlight, or lower your lights if you have a dimmer switch.

- Music: Incorporate soothing massage music, lullabies, and heartbeat sounds, which can all add to relaxation.

How Long Should You Expect the Massage to Last?

Depending on the time you have available, a full-body infant massage could last twenty to thirty minutes. Rushing or trying to fit massage in between other activities may unsettle your baby. If your baby does not engage or show any kind of relaxing emotion, or even if your baby starts crying, the massage is over. You cannot force your baby to relax. Try again when the baby is more receptive. Pick up your baby and give him or her a hug. Let your baby know it's okay.

- Remember, during the tummy massage your baby may cry and fuss if he or she has gas or is constipated. You can always pick your baby up and try burping during the tummy massage.

- Follow your baby's cues! Massage is supposed to be enjoyable for both of you.

- Remember, your baby is like a sponge. He can sense when you are stressed, tired, or in a hurry. If you are not relaxed, do not expect your baby to relax.

Introduction to Massage Techniques

These techniques should be performed slowly and smoothly to avoid overstraining the muscles.

It is advisable to massage on an empty stomach. Use an elevated position if the baby has been diagnosed with gastroesophageal reflux.

A newborn may hold tension in the abdomen. Do not be surprised if your baby cries or gets uncomfortable during the tummy massage. Picking up your baby during the tummy massage and burping well may help.

Pay attention to your baby's cues of engagement or disengagement. Infants respond in predictable ways and will let you know when they need time to rest. Do not overstimulate them.

It's okay if your baby falls asleep during the massage. It means baby is relaxed. Some babies do not like to be touched while they are asleep; if this is the case for your baby, then it will be best to continue the massage another time.

There is not a correct or incorrect place to start infant massage, or any massage for that matter, but you want it to flow from feet to head or head to toes. Personally, I like starting at the feet and ending on the back (which is the recommended flow of this textbook, but you could do it in reverse order if you wish).

No matter where you start, you always want to have continuous touch. For example, when kneading up the leg, you want to glide back down rather than kneading up the leg, taking your hand off, and then starting at the ankle again. This gives the baby a constant flow of energy.

What Oils or Lotions Should You Use?

You may or may not want to use massage oils or lotions on your baby. It is not required. You can give a massage with clothes on or off. Remember, babies lose heat quickly when they are uncovered. Make sure you keep the room warm.

- Allergy testing should be done with any new products you want to use on your baby. Your baby's skin is very sensitive.

- To be safe, place a small amount of oil or lotion on the inside of your baby's wrist. Wait twenty to thirty minutes. Check for any redness or a rash that might indicate a reaction.

- Avoid using any nut oils because your baby could have an allergic reaction.

- If no allergy is present, choose an unscented oil, which lets your baby bond with your natural scent first.

- Natural or organic oils (carrier oils) such as grapeseed, apricot, safflower, and jojoba work well. You can find these carrier oils at local health food stores.

- Avoid using mineral oil-based products. They do not absorb into the skin well, and they clog the pores.

How Much Pressure Should You Use?

You are actually going to use some pressure and move the skin. Massage strokes should be a medium yet gentle pressure. Medium pressure will be reassuring to your baby. Watch for any redness on the baby; it can indicate that you might need to lighten your touch. However, too light of a touch can be ticklish and aggravating, and then relaxation is out the window. Massage strokes are usually long, slow, and rhythmic. The massage strokes grow with the baby, using just enough pressure to be comfortable and relaxing.

Make It Unique

This is your own unique massage. Over time you'll find your favorite massage strokes and songs to accompany them. And of course, just saying "I love you" and your familiar touch will make this a unique experience for your baby. You may want to start slow by choosing several massage strokes. Then you can start adding more strokes as you become confident with the massage. As your child grows, the massage will grow with him or her.

Legs and Feet

Getting started: Choose either the right or the left leg. Do the following massage strokes on one leg, and then switch to the other leg and repeat the steps. Repeat each massage stroke three times.

1. Gently Massage Each Toe: Support the foot at the ankle with one hand; then, using the fingers of the other hand, gently massage by rubbing each toe in a circular motion, using a medium pressure, in case your baby is ticklish. If your baby seems to be ticklish, gently press each toe and rotate through each toe, starting with the big toe. Make sure to have good eye contact. You can also sing the nursery rhyme "This Little Piggy Went to Market."

2. Pressing Through the Bottom of the Foot: Using your thumb, press under the toes, the arch of the foot, and the heel. Apply medium to firm pressure versus light pressure in case your baby is ticklish.

3. Rotating the Ankle: Support the foot at the ankle with one hand, and then using your other hand, rotate the ankle to the right three times then to the left three times. Stretch the foot in a plantar flexion (down) and dorsal flexion (up) to stretch the Achilles tendon. This helps to stretch all the ligaments and tendons of the foot and ankle.

4. Circular Massage on Top of the Foot: Using both of your thumbs, apply circular massage on top of the foot. Press lightly, making a small circular motion. This helps promote good circulation and blood flow. You can also use your index finger or one thumb. (Dads may feel more comfortable using one rather than two.)

5. Effleurage to the Leg: Effleurage is a gliding stroke, long and smooth. Support the foot with one hand, and then using the other hand, starting at the outside of the ankle, make a "C" shape with your hand. Using medium pressure, roll in to the inner ankle, glide up the inner thigh, glide out to outer thigh, and glide back down to the ankle.

Note: You can also knead the leg in a circular motion. Starting at the ankle, begin kneading up the leg (like kneading dough) and gliding back down.

6. Wringing the Leg: Place one hand on the upper thigh and your other hand on the lower leg. Wrapping your hands around the leg, use gentle pressure and twist your hands in opposite directions. Use a *gentle* wringing motion back and forth. This motion is like wringing out a washcloth.

Note: Use a gentle motion; you don't want to twist too hard.

7. Fulling the Leg: Apply fulling compression movements. Fulling is a kneading technique in which the tissue is grasped and gently spread out. Start at the upper thigh. Place your thumbs in the middle of the upper thigh and press outward. Work down the thigh making three horizontal rows.

8. Rolling the Muscles of the Leg: Like playing with Play-Doh or Silly Putty, place your hands at mid-leg on each side, and gently roll the leg like you are making the Play-Doh into a rope shape. This is a very gentle rolling action with not a lot of pressure. If you are twisting the knee, you are using too much pressure or rolling action.

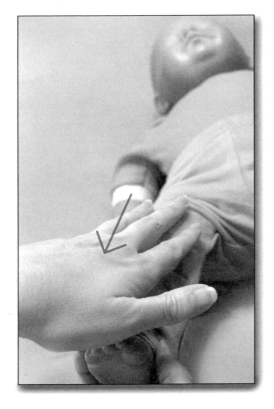

9. Feathering Down the Leg: Imagine your hand as a feather. Gently use a soft, featherlike stroke and move downward from the upper thigh to the ankle.

Tummy Massage

Getting started: Remember, the key to a happy baby is a happy tummy! Tummy massage is going to help reduce gas and constipation. Your baby will then have better feeding schedules, sleep longer, and should be happier.

In the first six to twelve weeks, parents have a tendency to feed their babies frequently, or even overfeed, when they see their babies sucking—they think baby is hungry, but this is not always the case. Sucking offers temporary pain relief. If your baby is gassy or colicky, he or she might want to suck on a pacifier or fingers. The baby is using this as a calming and soothing tool. Once breastfeeding is established, make sure you are allowing your baby's tummy time to digest.

Note: Remember to burp your baby all day every day, especially the first six to twelve weeks of life. They need help moving the gas or air bubbles up or down. Make sure you are using a firm burping technique. Love pats are not burping!

1. Sacral Release: At the lower spine, there are two dimpled indentions. Holding your baby in an upright position and using your index finger and middle finger, apply gentle pressure in the dimples. When gentle pressure is used on the sacrum, it triggers a sacral release. Sacral release relaxes the digestive system, allowing gas and waste to move through the digestive area without it feeling like a spastic colon would feel to us.

Note: Rocking, swaying, and bouncing relaxes the central nervous system. Add any of these when holding your baby. It takes three to five minutes for the central nervous system to relax. This can be combined with sacral release and burping all day, every day. It is very calming and soothing.

2. Clockwise Around the Tummy: Picture a clock sitting on your baby's tummy. The diaphragm is the twelve on the clock, and just below the navel is the six on the clock. On the right side going up is the ascending colon; going across the top is the transverse colon; and going down and emptying is the descending colon. Place your index and middle finger on the twelve (diaphragm) and apply circular massage around the clock (clockwise). This is how the colon flows. When you massage the tummy clockwise, you are helping the colon to empty.

3. Fulling the Tummy: Place your thumbs at the midline just below the baby's diaphragm. With your thumbs spreading outward to the baby's sides, make two rows, stopping just above the navel. Use a medium pressure. If your baby is gassy or constipated, you may want to apply a firmer pressure.

Note: This can be repeated all day to help calm the tummy, but remember to wait thirty to forty-five minutes after feedings. Typically, the tummy should be soft like a pillow. If the tummy feels hard or tight, your baby is gassy or needs to potty, which may make the massage uncomfortable. You can always pick your baby up for burping after any portion of the tummy massage and then proceed to the next step.

4. Let Your Fingers Do the Walking: Lay your baby on his or her left side. From the baby's right side, using your index finger and middle finger, walk your fingers across the tummy between the diaphragm and navel from right to left using medium pressure. This helps to move gas and waste through the colon. Also, placing your baby on his or her left side allows gravity to assist with digestion.

Note: If the baby appears to be gassy or has constipation, repeat the strokes several times a day.

5. Knee to Tummy Press: Supporting the ankles and knees, gently press the legs into the tummy and hold for three to five seconds. This is your baby's natural way of passing gas or moving waste.

6. Bicycle: Supporting the ankles and knees, gently bend one knee up to the abdomen and bring it back down. Then alternate with the other leg. Repeat the bicycle motion slowly and rhythmically a few times. This can help your baby pass gas.

Chest

Getting started: When working on the chest, arms, or face, you begin working in your baby's intimate space. If you notice your baby not wanting to make eye contact with you or turning his or her head away from you, simply change your position. Work from the side or turn your baby around so you are not working in a frontal position. This is also a great bonding massage. Make lots of eye contact and say, "I love you."

Repeat each massage stroke three times.

1. Shoulder Press: Gently cup your hands around your baby's shoulders. Looking into your baby's eyes, say, "Hello," and your baby's name. This is a great bonding tool!

2. Make a Heart Shape: Using your index fingers, outline a small shape of a heart on the baby's sternum. Making good eye contact, say, "I love you," and your baby's name.

Note: Make sure to keep the outline of the heart small. We want to teach our babies healthy touch. As our children grow, both girls and boys, if they have experienced healthy touch all of their lives, they will know when they are being touched inappropriately.

Arms and Hands

Getting started: Arm and hand massage creates good circulation, so start with either the right or left arm. Do all the massage strokes on one arm, and then switch to the other arm and repeat the steps.

Repeat each massage stroke three times.

1. Gently Massage Each Finger: Support the hand at the wrist with one hand, and then using the fingers of your other hand, gently massage and rotate through each finger using medium pressure, starting with the thumb.

2. Pressing Through the Palm of the Hand: Using your thumb, apply medium pressure and press below the fingers and all around the palm of the hand. You may also use circular massage on the palm of the hand.

3. Stretching of the Wrist: Support the hand at the wrist with one hand, and then using your other hand, gently rotate the wrist to the right three times then to the left three times.

4. Circular Massage on Top of the Hand: Using both of your thumbs, do small, circular massage on top of the hand, using a gentle to medium pressure. (Dads may want to use only one thumb.) This helps with circulation and blood flow.

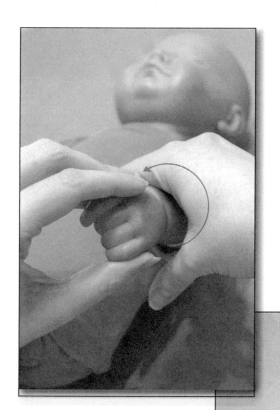

5. Effleurage to the Arm: Effleurage is a gliding stroke, long and smooth. Support the wrist with one hand, and then using the other hand, starting at the outside of the wrist, make a "C" shape with your hand. Using medium pressure, roll in to the inner wrist, glide up the inner arm, glide out to the outer arm, and glide back down to the wrist.

Note: You can also knead the arm in a circular motion. Starting at the wrist and using medium pressure, begin kneading (like dough) up the arm and glide back down.

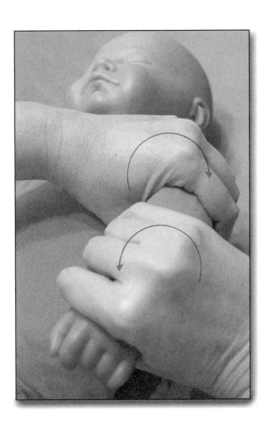

6. Wringing the Arm: Place one hand on the upper arm and the other hand on the lower arm. Use a *gentle*, wringing motion back and forth. This motion is like wringing out a washcloth.

7. Rolling the Muscles of the Arm: Place one hand on the upper arm and one hand on the lower arm. Again, like playing with Play-Doh or Silly Putty, begin rolling gently as if you are making the Play-Doh into a rope shape.

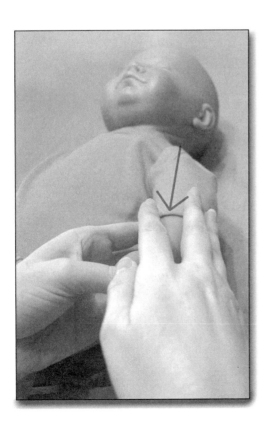

8. Feathering Down the Arm: Gently use a soft, feather-like stroke from the upper arm to the wrist, feathering off.

Face

Getting started: Looking into your baby's eyes and saying, "I love you," and your baby's name makes a very strong bond. Always look for ways to add this to your everyday life with your baby. Make sure to use light strokes with little or no oil for all facial massage.

Repeat each massage stroke three times.

1. Holding Your Baby's Head: Hold your baby's head gently in your hands. Making good eye contact, say, "I love you," and your baby's name.

2. Sweeping Over the Eyebrows: Using your thumbs, gently and with featherlike pressure, sweep over your baby's eyebrows. You can gently sweep over the forehead, up to the hairline, and back down the eyebrows.

3. Sweeping Over the Cheeks: Using your thumbs and with gentle, featherlike pressure, sweep across the cheeks to the outer face. You can also apply gentle, circular massage across the cheeks using your thumbs.

4. Circular Massage Around the Mouth: Using your index fingers, make small, gentle, circular massage motions around the outside of the mouth.

Note: Start this massage technique when your baby is an infant, and when your baby starts teething, he or she may allow you to massage around the mouth, which will increase blood flow and oxygen, therefore relieving pain.

You can even purchase a finger-toothbrush massager. Place this on your finger and do circular massage inside your baby's mouth over the baby's gums. This too will help with teething.

5. Sweeping Under the Chin: Using your thumbs, gently sweep along the jawline. You can also apply gentle circular massage along the jawline using your thumbs.

6. Massage the Ears: Using your thumbs and index fingers, gently lift the ears and apply circular massage around the outer edges of the ears.

7. Circular Scalp Massage: Using your fingertips, gently apply circular massage all over your baby's head.

Note: Be extra careful around the soft spot on the baby's head. Use very gentle pressure.

8. Sweeping the Baby's Head: Using the palm of your hand, starting from the forehead, make a gentle, featherlike sweep over the entire head to the neckline. Babies love this!

Back

Getting started: Place your baby across your lap. If you are still on the floor, it's best to cross your legs and lay the baby over your legs. If your baby is gassy or does not like tummy time, this may be uncomfortable. In that case, hold your baby up at your shoulder and work.

When working on the back, make sure the baby's head is supported. Until your baby can support his or her own head, you will have to hold the head with one hand and work with your other hand. **Never apply direct pressure to the spine!** It's okay to work on either side of the spine or glide over the spine.

Repeat each massage stroke three times.

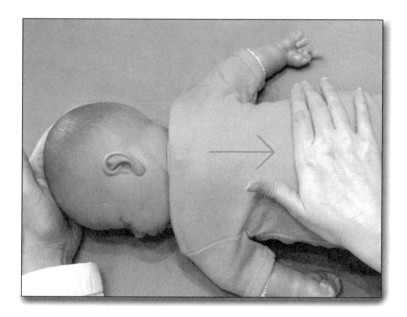

1. Gliding Down the Back: With the palm of your hand, start at your baby's neckline and use a gentle, featherlike sweeping motion as you glide down the back, stopping just at the hips.

2. Circular Massage: Using your fingertips, apply circular massage starting at the neckline and moving down one side of the spine to just above the hips three times. Switch sides and repeat.

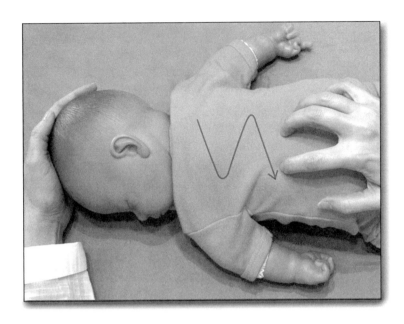

3. Zigzag Down the Back: Using your fingertips and starting at the neckline, gently zigzag down the back.

4. Scratching the Back: Using your fingertips, gently scratch the baby's back, starting at the neckline and working down the back.

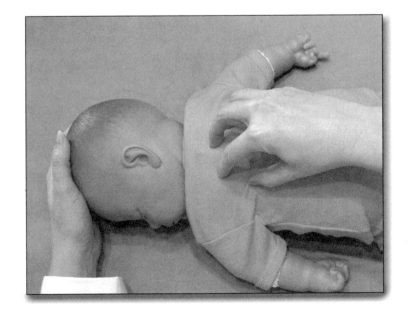

Conclusion

You have completed the full-body infant massage! Pick up your baby and give him or her a hug and a kiss. Say, "You did a great job!"

CPSIA information can be obtained
at www.ICGtesting.com
Printed in the USA
LVRC021026130919
630962LV00007B/171